Halloween Stories

R J Clarke

This book
belongs to

Contents

Introduction

For some children, October 31st is their favorite day of the year. It is a time when kids and grown ups all over the world dress up in scary costumes, share Halloween stories with each other and eat lots of candy!

Inside this exciting book, there are 50 short Halloween stories for children. Each story has a different theme with a variety of monsters and an ending that aims to delight.

Whether you're tucked up in bed or if you've just come back from your tricks and treats - this kids Halloween book can be enjoyed at any time!

Happy Halloween

The Ooga Booga Monster

As I was brushing my teeth and getting ready for bed, my big brother told me all about the Ooga Booga monster. He seemed to know an awful lot about what it looked like and he knew exactly what the Ooga Booga monster wanted. It wanted to snatch small children from their beds at night.

I didn't believe a word he said until in the middle of the night, I just so happened to see the Ooga Booga monster walk into my bedroom. Its ugly face was exactly how my big brother described.

I didn't want the monster to catch me looking at it so I pulled the duvet up to cover my face. I now believed that the monster couldn't see me and I felt a bit safer.

However, I wasn't sure if the Ooga Booga monster was still in my bedroom or not. So after an uneventful minute under my duvet, I peeked out from the covers.

I couldn't see the Ooga Booga monster anywhere. I even checked under my bed and nothing was there.

The Ooga Booga monster had mysteriously vanished and it meant that I could get back to sleep again.

When the morning arrived, I was going to tell my mom and dad that I saw the Ooga Booga monster and I was going to ask them to help me to keep the monster away.

However, on my way downstairs I saw a mask on a table and it had the same ugly face as the Ooga Booga monster. I then realized that there was no monster last night - it was just my big brother wearing a mask.

The little white ghost

My mom shouted from another room, "Can you help me with the laundry?" I selfishly shouted back, "No, I'm playing a video game".

I was on a really tricky level in my game and it required my full concentration. However, I couldn't give it because my pet dog Scooby started to lick my hand. I laughed uncontrollably, "Stop it, that tickles".

Suddenly my video game character died. Luckily, I still had two more lives left. So in order to make the most out of them, I sent Scooby out of the room and shut the door behind him so that he couldn't get back in and disturb me.

I turned my game back on but my brain didn't react quickly enough, causing my character to die again.

I spoke to myself; "I'll do better at this game if I have some more energy inside of me". I was feeling a little hungry by now anyway so I got my butt off my comfy chair and headed towards the door to get a snack.

However, when I opened the door, a little white ghost came running towards me. In a poor attempt to escape, I tripped over myself and landed backwards on to the floor.

I closed my eyes and the ghost was suddenly on top of me and it was licking my face.

I opened my eyes and I realized that it wasn't a ghost at all. It was just Scooby who must have got himself trapped under a sheet from when my mom was doing the laundry.

Gorilla

The walls in my house must be thin because one evening I overheard my mom tell my older brother who was downstairs; "I hope you enjoy your party tonight". "Oh, I will" he chuckled.

The front door slammed shut and I came rushing to it. I saw my mom by the door and I asked, "Did somebody say party? I like parties. Can I go? Please?" My mom frowned, "You're not going anywhere until you get all of your homework done". I tried to reason, "But it's Halloween". My mom replied, "Well you should have done your homework yesterday then".

I hung my head low as I trotted back upstairs where I soon slumped at my desk. It took me hours to complete all of my homework but I finally did it and I felt great. I knew that I was free to go out but I only had ten minutes left before it was my bedtime. I thought that I should at least get some fresh air tonight so I opened the front door and I was looking forward to seeing the neighbors Halloween decorations.

However, I didn't even get to the top of my driveway before a giant gorilla was chasing me back into my house. I ran into the house as fast I could but the gorilla followed me in. It even followed me up the stairs and having nowhere to go, I then curled into a ball in the corner of my bedroom. I watched in horror as the gorilla waved its arms around and beat its chest.

It then started to laugh and I realized that it must be my older brother wearing a fancy dress costume, as gorillas don't laugh.

Hide and Seek

I asked my dad what type of job he had and he replied, "I'm a biology teacher". I thought it was cool how he knew all about how the human body works. I told him, "When I grow up I want to be just like you".

He smiled and I then asked my dad if he wanted to play a game of hide and seek with me. He closed his eyes and said, "OK" and he started to count down from 30.

As I was looking for a good hiding spot, I noticed a closet door that was usually locked was now open. I thought I'd go in there.

I laughed to myself, "He'll never find me in here". Ten minutes had passed and my legs were starting to ache. So I leaned against a wall but I touched something strange.

Since it was so dark, I couldn't see what it was but as my hand reached back and touched it more, it felt like it was a skeleton.

I jumped out of the closet and I saw with my own two eyes that it was indeed a skeleton. Was it someone who was never found in a game of hide and seek. I did not know. Was the skeleton alive? Again, I did not know.

I screamed and my dad came rushing in to the room. He asked, "What's the matter?" I pointed, "There's a skeleton in your closet".

He laughed, "It's not a real one. It's made out of plastic see". He gave it a few taps on the head and I started to calm down. I realized that it must be something that my dad uses as a prop to teach the children in his biology class.

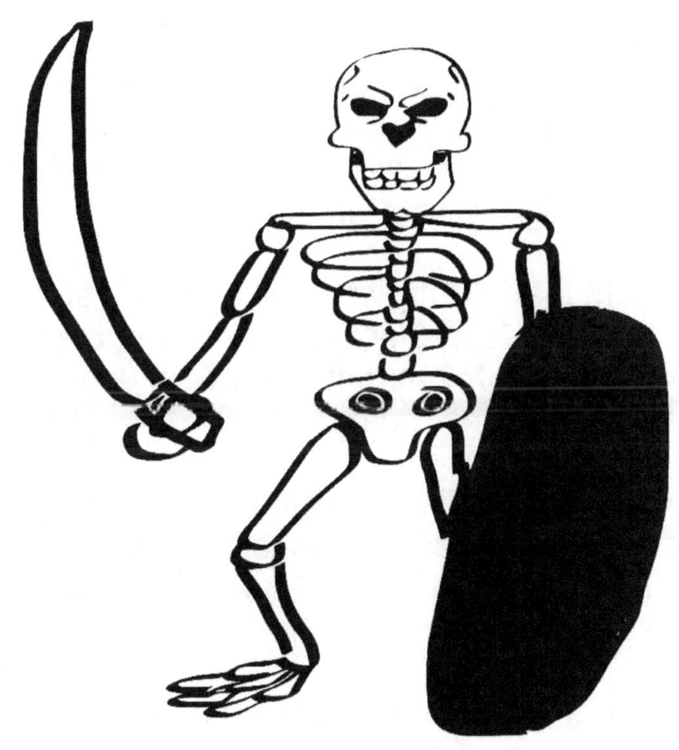

Mummy

My mom muttered, "I can't believe we have ran out of it already. I want you and your brother to be on your best behavior while I'm gone to do a shop. I won't be long, OK".

When my mom left the house, my brother disappeared upstairs. I had a feeling that he was up to no good so I decided to go into his bedroom. However, he wasn't there.

I looked in my bedroom, the spare room and the bathroom but he wasn't there either. I concluded that he must be in our parent's bedroom. But it was a place that our parents had forbidden us to go into.

I thought that as long as I don't actually step into the room, I wouldn't get in any trouble. So I slowly opened my parent's bedroom door and I peeked inside the room.

I couldn't believe it. My brother was standing in our parent's bedroom. I walked in and I was about to tell him that I had caught him doing something naughty.

However, my brother wasn't the only person in the room. Lying on top of the bed was an Egyptian mummy.

I uttered, "Oh sugar". My words woke the mummy up and I was the first thing that it saw.

The mummy got up and it seemed to be really angry with me. It ran after me but when I turned around, I saw that it had hairy arms. I realized that it wasn't a mummy at all - it was my daddy who was just wrapped up in toilet roll. It also looked like I was going to get the blame for my brother's prank.

The many eyed monster

My mom told me, "Come here a minute. I want to tell you something. Grandma is staying a few nights in our spare room". I was delighted and jumped in joy at the news.

My mom warned, "Grandma has trouble sleeping at night so I don't want you and your brother waking her up with your petty squabbles".

I said, "I will be on my best behavior. It's my brother that you have to worry about". My mom said, "Right. I'm going to get grandma now. I'll be back soon".

I told my brother about grandma staying but his head was inside his monster book. I asked, "What are you reading?" He replied, "About how the many eyed monster takes away your eyeballs".

I didn't want to know anything more about that monster but he told me all about it anyway, laughing when he got to the gory bits!

When my mom came back home, I knew that my grandma would be there too so I rushed over and greeted her but she looked very tired.

My mom said, "It's really late, you should both be in bed by now". We went to bed soon after without any squabbling.

When the morning arrived, I stretched my arms and yawned but when I opened my eyes, everything was black. I thought, "Oh, no. I can't see. I'm blind".

I feared that the monster my brother told me about had taken away my eyeballs. Then when I touched where my eyes should have been, I felt something strange.

I felt fabric and I realized that it was just a blindfold. My brother must have taken it from my grandma when she was asleep.

Zombie

I decided to skip supper one night and my mom told me, "Don't blame me if you get hungry".

As I went to bed on an empty stomach, I drifted off to sleep just as quick as normal. However, my grumbling stomach woke me up during the night and when I looked at my alarm clock to see what time it was, I couldn't believe it. It was only half past two in the morning.

I knew that I would struggle to get back to sleep with my stomach grumbling as much as it was so I decided to go downstairs to get something to eat.

Since I didn't want to wake anyone else up, I trod quietly and I didn't switch any lights on.

Through the darkness, I grabbed hold of the banister and I patted the walls so that I could tell where I was going. As I finally got to the kitchen, I opened the fridge door and it lit up the room ineffectively.

I could make out a large figure in the room and I asked, "Who's there?" It made a grunting noise and then it held out its arms like a zombie and walked very slowly towards me.

I quickly put the kitchen light on and when I came to my senses, I realized that it wasn't a zombie, it was my dad and he was sleep walking. It's a good job the front door is locked at night.

Witch

My older brother told me that he had heard someone say that the woman living next-door was a witch.

I told my brother, "But I'm friends with the girl next-door and she has invited me around her house tonight".

My brother laughed menacingly before telling me, "If you do go then you might come back as a frog".

I gulped. I didn't want to be a frog but I didn't want to let my friend down either. In the end I decided to go to my friends house because if I didn't go then the witch might get mad and I'd definitely be turned into a frog.

When I knocked on my next-door neighbor's house, my knock pushed the door wide open and I saw a big black cauldron.

I was ready to turn around but then the witch who was living there came from behind me and led me inside. She said, "Make yourself at home and I'll just get my daughter". I thought to myself, "Daughter? That must make her my friend's mother".

As I waited, I looked around the room and I saw a broomstick, a lot of potions on a shelf and a bunch of frogs in a tank

My friend came down the stairs and said, "What's the matter, you look like you've seen a ghost". I told her what my older brother had said to me and she laughed.

She then explained that the broomstick was for cleaning, the bottles of potions were medicine and the frogs were her pets.

Soon afterwards, her mother gave us a spoonful of liquid from her cauldron to try and it tasted just like soup. I realized that the cauldron was just a big pot and that the woman wasn't a witch, it was just a misunderstanding fed by my brother's active imagination.

Wolf

I had a dream about having another dog. It was brown just like our Scooby and they played together and got on really well with each other.

On coming out of the dream, I wished the dream was true and it gave me an idea to ask my mom and dad if we could have another dog.

It was really early but I knew that my dad would be having his breakfast by now so I went downstairs to ask him.

He said, "One dog is enough. You should be grateful that we have Scooby".

I said, "Where is Scooby? He normally comes to me when I get up". My dad said, "He's just in the living room and there's something I should tell you first".

Instead of listening to my dad, I walked into the living room and I saw Scooby. However, I also saw a wolf.

I bolted out of the room, ran upstairs and shut my bedroom door. A whole hour had passed and I still didn't dare come out.

My mom shouted, "Why aren't you coming down?" I replied, "Because there's a wolf down there". She yelled, "No there isn't".

She didn't believe me. So I went downstairs with her to show the wolf to her. I carefully opened the living room door and there it was.

My mother wasn't afraid though and I quickly realized that my parents were just pet sitting a Husky. Maybe next time my dad tries to tell me something, I will listen.

Invisible

It was Saturday; my favorite day of the week and my older brother had invited his best friend over.

My brother was talking to his friend about what super powers they would like. I joined in their conversation and said that I wished that I could have the power of invisibility.

My brother looked around and said, "Did you hear something?" His friend shook his head and my brother continued, "Yeah you're right it was probably nothing".

I said in a louder tone of voice, "I'm right here. How can you not hear me?" Neither of them answered me. I started to believe that my wish of having invisibility had come true. This was because they couldn't see me and nor could they hear me.

I thought it would be funny to see their reaction when I pick an object up so I lifted a glass from a table. They looked at it and said, "Whoa, check it out, the glass is floating".

His friend said, "Dude, I think your house is haunted". My brother said, "Yeah it must be. If I was a ghost I would walk through walls".

I thought, "Hey, that's not a bad idea, maybe I'll try that". So I ran into the wall but for some reason I didn't go through. I just ended up hurting myself.

They both laughed at me. Then I realized that my brother and his friend were only pretending that I was an invisible ghost. I later learned that all super powers have their downsides too.

Pumpkin carving

I had always wanted to do some pumpkin carving so when I finally got a big pumpkin, I scooped the inside out with a spoon and I began using a knife to cut out a face.

My brother kept telling me, "It needs to look scarier". I gave it sharper teeth and made its eyes look more evil but it still wasn't scary enough for my brother.

Not long after, my dad came into the living room and said, "You've been doing that all this afternoon. Why don't you take a break? We could go out to see a movie if you want?"

I put the knife down, slipped on my trainers and told my dad about all of the latest movies that I wanted to watch.

My dad asked my brother if he wanted to come with us but he refused. He said, "I don't want to watch some stupid kids movie. I'm too old for that".

I had a great time with my dad and we were quite full after eating a tub of popcorn.

When we came back home, it was dark and there was an eerie glow coming from the living room. I decided to take a look.

What I saw shocked me. It was not human. This thing was huge and it had an evil grin on its black face.

I immediately faced away but then I took a second look and it started to look familiar. I realized that it was just a shadow coming from my pumpkin, which now had a candle inside.

Bed bugs

My brother had just returned from our back garden and he had a handful of red berries.

I asked him, "Why have you been picking so many berries?" He replied, "It's none of your business". He ran upstairs, presumably into his bedroom where he liked to spend most of his time.

When the day was coming to an end, I tucked myself into bed as I was old enough to do it myself now.

Moments later, my brother opened my bedroom door and he said, "Sleep tight, don't let the bed bugs bite". He had never said that to me before and I now couldn't stop thinking about bed bugs biting me.

I had not been in bed for more than a minute and I had an itch, which was soon followed by another and another.

It felt like I had bed bugs crawling all over me. The more I wriggled, the more places I itched.

I knew that I wouldn't be able to see the bed bugs as they are too small to see but I put the light on anyway.

I was surprised at what I saw. There was all this red powder scattered on my bed. I realized that there weren't any bed bugs in my bed, it was just itching powder and I knew of only one person naughty enough to create it – my brother! So that's what the berries were for...

Gnomes

It was a sunny day so I went in my back garden to play with some toy dinosaurs.

I set them all up on a rockery and I talked to them and treated them as if they were alive.

I was all by myself although I didn't feel like it because behind me, there were some creepy garden gnomes on the lawn.

All of the gnomes were statues of little old men with pointy red hats and I didn't like them looking at me.

I tried to pretend that they weren't there and I carried on playing with my toy dinosaurs.

However, when I wasn't looking at the gnomes, they must have been walking towards me. This is because when I turned around, they were closer to me than I last remembered.

On the times when I did look at them, they were as still as statues. It was so weird.

By now, the garden gnomes were really close
to me and I didn't know if they were friendly or
not. Sure, they had friendly smiles but there
was something about them that gave me the
creeps.

I continued to play with my toy dinosaurs for a
brief moment before turning around. I saw
movement this time but it wasn't a gnome, it
was my brother.

He was touching one of the gnomes and I
realized that the gnomes weren't alive. It was
just my brother trying to fool me by moving
them around. My brother can be very mean.

Poltergeist

I was in my garden helping my mom to hang the washing on the line. I liked being helpful and my mom appreciated the help.

As I was fiddling with a peg, I questioned, "How will the clothes dry when there is no sun out?" She replied, "Oh, it will dry, I have checked the weather forecast and it is going to be perfect for drying clothes".

I never saw the sun come out that whole day and when nighttime came, I went to bed and I tried to think of happy thoughts.

No matter how hard I tried to get to sleep, I couldn't do it. I kept hearing noises and I wasn't sure what or who was making them.

I heard noises like tapping, scratching and hissing. There was also a loud crashing sound at one point.

When I told my brother about it in the morning, he teased, "It sounds like a poltergeist to me. They are similar to ghosts but they can move objects around".

I stormed out of the room and when I looked out of a window, I saw that there were lots of things in the garden that were blown over.

I then realized that the sounds that I heard last night weren't a poltergeist - it was just the wind moving the washing and trees around.

The Headless Horseman

One day, I went to visit a stable and as I was stroking a horse on its head, my brother said, "Have you heard about the headless horseman?" I shook my head.

My brother continued, "Apparently he lost his head when it was hit by a cannonball a long time ago. He now goes out every night and he searches for his head".

I told my brother, "That doesn't sound so scary". But then he said, "Since the headless horseman still hasn't found his head, there is a rumor that he is looking to replace it with someone else's head".

I held tightly on to my head, "Nobody is taking away my head". He said, "I wouldn't be so sure about that if I were you".

He was grinning as he wandered off. Fortunately, the horse was keeping me calm but I had to leave the horse behind when my dad called, "Come on, we've got to head back home now".

When we got home, I went straight into my bedroom to listen to some music. As I was dancing to the beat, I looked at my doorway.

The headless horseman was standing there and I screamed really loud. However, my mom and dad probably didn't hear me over my loud music.

When I took a breath, I soon recognized that the headless horseman was wearing the same t-shirt as my brother. I then realized that it wasn't the headless horseman at all - it was just my brother who had put his head inside his t-shirt.

Slime monster

The first thing that I used to do when I came home from school was to play with some slime. I enjoyed stretching it, squeezing it and poking it. I found it oddly satisfying but nobody else in my family could understand why.

One day, my brother saw me kneading it and he told me, "You shouldn't be touching that".

When I asked him why, he reasoned, "Because it looks like something that dripped off a slime monster. You do know that it'll come back for it don't you?"

I started to wonder if he was right and if what I was holding in my hands was a part of a monster.

Before I went to bed, I left my slime downstairs just in case the monster was real.

However, when it was completely black in my bedroom, I saw a glowing green slimy blob floating towards me. I said quietly to myself, "Oh no, I forgot to wash my hands and I must still have some of that slime on my fingers".

I put my lamp on and I quickly realized that it wasn't a floating slimy monster at all. It was just my brother holding my slime and now I knew that it could glow in the dark, which was actually pretty awesome.

Sewer alligators

As I was in the bathroom using the toilet, my brother knocked on the door and he shouted, "Hurry up!"

Since we only had one toilet in our house, we all had to learn to share it. The problem was that my brother didn't like sharing anything.

As he waited behind the door, he asked me, "Did you know that there are alligators living in the sewers?"

I said, "No, why do you ask?" He replied, "Oh it's probably nothing to worry about. It's just that the toilet leads to the sewer".

I started to worry that an alligator would come up the toilet and bite me on my bottom. So I hurried up and let my brother have a turn in the bathroom.

Then I thought about all of the lies that my brother had told me in the past. So I decided to ask my mom if alligators live in the sewers. She shocked me when she said, "It's true, they do".

Later on in the day, I needed to go to the toilet again. I tried to hold it in because I was too scared to go. When I could hold it no longer, I decided to take the risk.

However, before sitting down on the toilet seat, I looked at the toilet and all of its pipes. I realized that I was safe after all because an alligator could never fit through a toilet cistern pipe, surely not.

Possessed

It was the school holidays and my friend Riley invited me to a sleepover. I stayed in a tent with Riley and Sam in the back garden and we stayed up really late playing Dungeons & Dragons.

Eventually, we went to sleep but I happened to wake up in the middle of the night and Riley was snoring.

Then all of a sudden, Riley said, "Where's my pitchfork?"

I said in a partially afraid voice, "Riley - what are you talking about?" Riley replied in a deep voice, "My name is not Riley. It's the devil".

Riley then started snoring immediately afterwards. I wished I could go to sleep that quickly but I couldn't because I was too frightened.

I thought that Riley must be possessed by the devil.

When the morning arrived, I told Riley and Sam what had happened but they didn't believe me.

When I looked at the game we were playing last night, I remembered that Riley was playing as a devil character. I then realized that Riley must have been sleep talking last night.

Carnivorous plant

One day my brother asked me to come into his room. This was highly unusual as he usually tells me to go away. However, I went in and he showed me a strange looking plant.

He asked me, "Do you know what this is?" I shrugged my shoulders because I didn't have a clue. He then told me, "It's a carnivorous plant".

My brother continued to ask me, "Do you know what carnivores eat?" I said, "Meat". He nodded, "That's right and guess what you are made out of?" I gulped, "Meat".

He then looked at his plant and said, "I think it's hungry".

I was truly terrified because I thought that my brother was thinking about feeding me to his plant.

My worst fears came true when he grabbed hold of my finger and aimed it at one of its many mouths.

I shouted, "Let go of me" but he did not listen. He then stuck my finger in a plant's mouth and its teeth started closing on my finger.

Fortunately, I looked at the plant's label and it said it was a Venus flytrap. I then realized that I was safe because the plant only ate flies.

Snow monster

It was the hottest day of the year and I went to the freezer to make myself some ice cream. However, I couldn't open the drawer. It was frozen shut.

I complained to my mom about it but she said, "Not right now, I'm too busy doing other household chores".

So in order to cool down, I challenged my brother to a water gun fight. We had hours of fun and we completely drenched each other.

On our way back to the house, I noticed that there was a mound of snow. I said out loud, "That's strange. We shouldn't have any snow when it's this hot".

My brother looked at the snow and he said, "Yep. It is just as I feared. We got a snow monster on the loose and it's probably still somewhere in our garden".

I ran back inside the house and I wanted some comfort food more than ever. So I tried to open the freezer again to get an ice cream.

The draw slid open easily this time around. I then realized that there was no snow monster outside - it was just the ice from the freezer, which my mom must have cleared out while we were playing.

Grim Reaper

My dad asked my brother to help him with some gardening. My brother selfishly asked, "What's in it for me?" My dad replied, "I will let you use one of my tools".

I asked my dad, "Can I use one of your tools?" He said politely, "Sorry sweet pea, you're just not old enough yet".

As my dad and brother went out, it gave me an opportunity to look at my brother's most prized possession - his monster book.

It was already turned on a page about the Grim Reaper so I sat by the window and I started to read. I found out what the Grim Reaper looked like and I discovered much about him including that he was also called Death.

I read a lot and I would have continued to read more had there not been three knocks on our front door.

Since I was the closest to the door, I answered it. I was shocked when I saw that it was someone very tall, dressed in black and holding a scythe.

I had no doubt in my mind that it was the Grim Reaper. It matched the picture and description in my brother's book perfectly.

I begged, "I don't want to die. I'm too young to die. Please don't kill me".

As I lowered my head to the ground, I saw the Grim Reaper's feet. They weren't the bony skeleton feet I expected. They looked like they were wooden sticks.

I quickly realized that it wasn't the Grim Reaper - it was just my brother on stilts and he was wearing my dad's coat and carrying a garden tool. My brother laughed, "That will teach you for reading my book".

Medusa

I had just recently learned about Greek mythology at school and I found it very interesting. On a car trip into town, I told my mom and dad all about the Greek Gorgons Euryale, Stheno and Medusa.

When we finally got into the town, we visited a shop. However, when we came out, I noticed that there was a statue of a man in the middle of the street.

I knew for sure that he wasn't there before. It was as if he had just been turned into stone on the spot and I knew of only one thing that could do such a thing. It had to be Medusa.

Since I knew that anyone who looked into Medusa's eyes would turn into stone, I kept my head down and I looked at the floor. I also used the reflection of shop windows to see where Medusa could be but I couldn't see her anywhere.

I warned my parents to be careful but they didn't seem to know the danger they were in. I told them both, "Weren't you listening to a word I was saying when we were in the car".

My dad then put some money into a box next to the feet of the statue. It suddenly came back to life. I then realized that he wasn't turned into stone - he was just a street performer. He was also a very nice man who gave me his Frisbee.

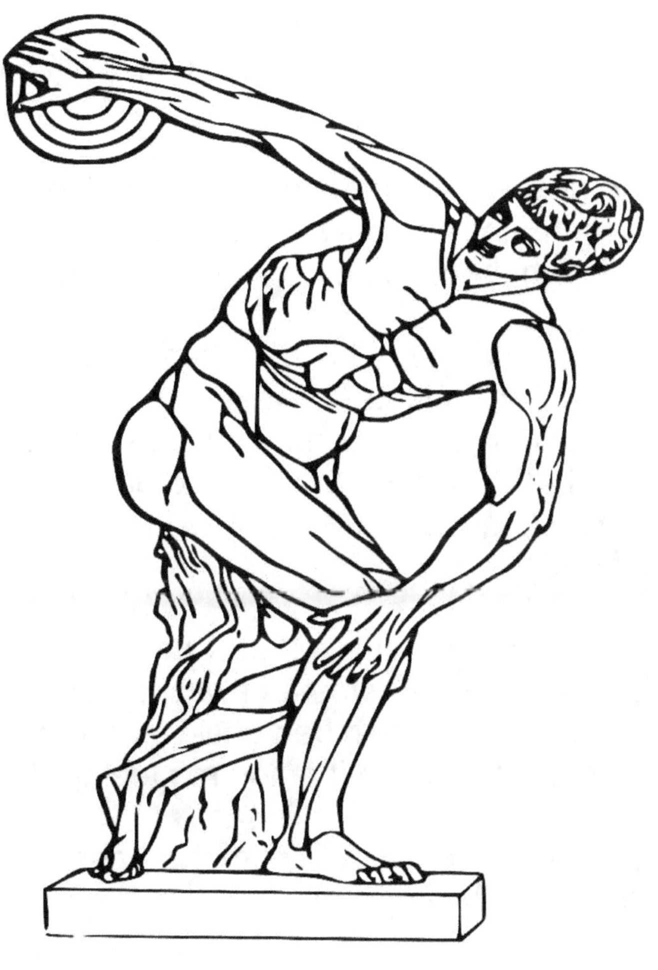

Werewolf

I sat on the edge of my seat as I watched a TV program about werewolves. I learned that they looked just like humans but that they change into a monster when there is a full moon.

It just so happened that there was a full moon outside my house too. This made watching the TV program very scary.

During a tense moment, my mom burst into the living room and she said, "Bedtime". It gave me such a fright because it was so unexpected.

Once I calmed down, I told my mom, "OK, I'll be coming up in a minute". Five minutes had passed and my mom came into the room again. She said, "Come on, you've got to get up early for school tomorrow". I said, "I just need to see how it ends".

My mom crossed her arms because she wasn't happy that I wasn't doing as I was told. She then said, "I can't go to bed until you do". She then left the room and it made me feel guilty.

My eyes were heavy but I somehow continued to watch the TV program.

After a while, I saw my mom come into the room again but this time, she turned into a werewolf. Her body was all hairy and her fingernails turned into sharp claws.

She then jumped on top of me and raked her claws across my stomach. My pajamas were ripped to shreds.

My eyes were closed as my mom said, "Go to bed". I then saw that she was now human and that she was standing by the door. I checked my body and there was no scratch marks and my pajamas were not ripped either. I realized that it was just a nightmare and that I really should go to bed.

Hand

It was the school holidays and my dad and his work friends were building a new driveway for us.

There was a big pile of sand that I desperately wanted to play with but my dad told me, "Sorry kiddo, this sand isn't suitable for playing with".

I asked, "Why not?" He replied, "It's very gritty and it'll be too rough on your hands".

I was disappointed but then I had an idea. I quietly told myself, "I will just get a spade".

When I returned to the pile of sand with my pink spade, I saw a man's hand sticking out of the sand. I thought that someone must have been buried alive.

I thought about trying to dig them out but I thought that would take forever. So instead I reached to pull them out and even though I knew that I wasn't very strong, I thought that I would at least try.

I tugged as hard as I could and ended up pulling the man's hand off. I was horrified but then I soon realized that it wasn't a human's hand - it was just a mannequin's hand and someone must have put it there for a joke.

Spider

I went trick or treating with my older brother. He didn't like that I was with him though and he often reminded me, "You're cramping my style and you're only with me because dad said I couldn't go alone".

I started to cry. He said, "Don't cry, I didn't mean to hurt your feelings. I'm sorry". He then cheered me up by telling me about all of the candy we will both get if we work together.

We then went from one house to the next and said, "Trick or treat". They all gave us candy and complimented our outfits. My brother wore his Ooga Booga mask and I dressed up as a little devil.

When we returned home, we had a bucket full of candy but when I reached in to get a handful, I pulled out a huge spider.

I screamed and ran out of the room. After a while, I gained the courage to go back into the room and I asked, "Is it gone?" My brother had his hand in his pocket as he replied, "Don't worry, it's gone now".

I noticed that my bucket of candy was half empty whilst my brother's was now overflowing. I said, "This doesn't look right. I'm telling mom".

He pleaded, "Don't be a baby. I'll put them back". As he was tipping his bucket into mine, a spider slipped out of his pocket.

I screamed again but then I realized that it wasn't real - it was just a rubber spider. I still didn't like it though and I complained, "I'm still telling mom". My brother sighed at this and added more candy to my bucket. One point to me!

Robot invasion

I was sitting at the dining room table drawing a picture of a robot. The outline was complete and I just needed to use a crayon to fill it in neatly within the lines.

My brother saw my unfinished picture and he told me, "Robots will take over the world one day you know. It is only a matter of time before they rise up and turn everyone into slaves".

I said, "That won't happen, surely not". However, he seemed certain about it, "It will happen and it will happen sooner than you think". He then left the room, which left me thinking about it.

When I finished my drawing, I went upstairs to hang it up in my bedroom. But when I turned around, a tiny robot was walking into my bedroom. I thought, "Oh, no. The invasion is starting".

I jumped on top of my bed and I watched in terror as its little metal feet were slowly making their way towards me.

Since I didn't want to be captured and turned into a slave, I leaped over it and I ran out of my bedroom.

Fortunately, I bumped into my brother who was holding a joystick. I then realized that there was no robot invasion, at least not yet anyway - it was just a remote controlled robot and my brother was trying to scare me with it.

UFO

I was in the garden at night with my dad and we were playing with a glow in the dark Frisbee.

I suddenly noticed that there was a bright light in the night sky. I asked my dad, "What is that?"

He rubbed his chin before saying, "I don't know darling but I can tell you that it isn't a star because stars don't move and it isn't an airplane either because their lights blink".

As I held the Frisbee in my little hands, I came to the conclusion, "It's a UFO". I then pleaded, "Can we follow it".

My dad meanly said, "No". Then he looked at my teary eyes and he said, "OK we'll follow it for a little while if it'll make you happy".

Moments later, I jumped into his car and we chased after it. We were getting close to the UFO but then it suddenly dropped out of the sky and crashed.

I asked my dad to go over there to make sure that the alien flying the UFO was not hurt.

When we arrived at the crash site, I realized that it wasn't a UFO - it was just the burnt out remains of a Chinese flying lantern. Maybe one day I will see a real UFO.

Alien

My dad had just picked me up in his car from my after school dance lessons. It was the only time that I was able to be a front seat passenger and I liked it a lot.

Not only did I have a good view of the road, I could also recline my seat.

As I was looking ahead, I thought that it was strange that we weren't heading back home in the normal way. I didn't say anything because we had the radio on and it was a tune my dad really liked.

Eventually, we stopped in a car park and he told me that he'd be back soon. However, I ended up waiting ages and I became very bored.

As I was looking in the car mirror, I heard someone get into the back seat of the car. I turned around and I saw a green alien sitting there and it was wearing a seat belt.

In a mad panic, I jumped out and luckily my dad was on his way back to the car. I ran to my dad and I told him about the alien but he just laughed.

I stared through the car window and the green alien was now sitting in my seat at the front of the car.

The alien's hairstyle looked familiar and I realized that it wasn't a real alien - it was just my brother with green makeup on. He then explained that he had just come from his first day at drama club.

Wizard

My parents had taken me to a place packed full of people. My dad said, "Get ready to be amazed".

The next thing I knew, a wizard came on to a stage and he had a really long white beard. He brought with him a big wooden box and I wondered what it was for.

The wizard announced to the audience, "I need a volunteer". A little boy similar to my age put his hand up and the wizard chose him to get up on to the stage.

The wizard then said to everyone, "I'm going to make this boy disappear". He led him into the box and closed the door. After the wizard said, "Abracadabra" and opened the door, the boy was gone.

The wizard then said, "Who else shall I make disappear". Nobody put their hand up but I saw a few fingers pointed at me.

The wizard briefly looked around and then he picked me. So I walked on to the stage and entered the box. I didn't dare refuse what he asked me to do because I knew how powerful the wizard was.

The wizard then said. "Abracadabra" and I fell through a trap door under the stage. I landed on something soft and then I realized that it wasn't real magic - it was just a magic trick.

Cemetery

One day, I was walking through a cemetery with my family. I liked looking at all of the different gravestones and thought about what I would want mine to look like.

Some of them were in different shapes, some were crumbling into dust and there were some that had pretty flowers next to them.

I then saw a gravestone with a big hole in front of it and I said to my brother, "This must be for someone new".

My brother got close to the gravestone and he said, "It's got your name written on it". At first, I thought that he was joking but when I got closer, I realized that he was right".

My brother then teased, "It must be for you. Why else do you think mom and dad brought us here?"

I started to get really worried. I said to myself, "It can't be true".

I went back to the gravestone with my name on it but when I read some more, I noticed that the birth year was different to mine. I then realized that the name on the gravestone was just a coincidence. I guess because my name is quite common that I will see many more gravestones with my name on them.

Gunshot

I was playing in the park with my brother. We went on swings, a slide and a seesaw and we were getting along with each really well.

However, when I watched my brother use the monkey bars, I heard a really loud bang.

My brother suddenly dropped to the ground and he clutched his chest. I ran over to him and I could tell that he was in pain.

He said, "I've just been shot". His eyes soon closed and he looked dead.

I was so upset that I cried over his dead body. Then a thought came into my head. I said, "I know, I will give you the kiss of life".

My brother's eyes suddenly opened and he said, "Actually, I'm feeling much better now".

He stood up and dusted the dirt off his clothes. He quietly muttered, "I'm never doing that again". I said, "Sorry, I couldn't quite hear you". He told me, "I was just saying how glad I was to dodge that bullet".

Then when I heard more gunshots, I looked to see where they were coming from. I looked at the sky and I realized that it was just a firework display. It was spectacular and I forgot all about my brother's stunt.

Men in Black

I went into a shopping mall with my parents and I wore a hoodie but with the hood down. I asked my mom and dad if I could go to a stationary store and they bought me some new crayons.

Since coming out of the store, I noticed that there were some Men in Black following me around the shopping mall.

From listening to my brother at breakfast that day, I knew that the Men in Black are secret government agents that can wipe people's memories.

I wasn't sure what I had seen for them to want to wipe my memory clean but I was quite fond of my memories so I wanted to protect them.

I put my hood up to hide my identity but in doing so I felt something hard in my hood. It was a ruler.

I looked at the ruler and I said, "How did this get there?" I thought about it and I concluded that it must have dropped into my hood when I was in the stationary store.

I returned the ruler to the shop and it was a good job too because when I looked at the badge that the Men in Black were wearing, I realized that they were security guards.

Egyptian curse

My brother told me that there was supposed to be a really ancient artifact in the attic and that is was supposed to be extremely valuable.

I questioned, "Why hasn't anybody gone up to get it?" My brother said, "Because nobody has dared to go up into the attic".

I said, "Well, I'm brave enough to do it". My brother grinned as he gave me a torch and then he set the ladders up for me.

I climbed up the attic and I called down, "What am I looking for?" He said, "It looks like a black cat".

I found the figurine within the darkness and I wiped the cobwebs off it. I felt so proud but when I went to hand it over to my brother he said, "I don't want to touch that - it's got an Egyptian curse on it".

I was horrified. My brother had tricked me into getting cursed. It was the worst thing he had ever done to me and I was very angry with him.

However, as I looked at the underside of the black cat, I saw a sticker that read, "Made in China". I then realized that it didn't come from an ancient Egyptian tomb. It came from China and so there wasn't a curse. My brother just made it up.

Germs

My whole family went to visit my granddad at the hospital. He wasn't feeling very well but he was getting better.

After an hour, my brother needed to use the restroom. When he got back, we started to leave the hospital and I noticed that there were a lot of signs on the walls.

I scratched my head as I wondered what they meant.

My brother saw me looking at them and he told me, "They are warnings about germs. You don't want to touch them germs or else you will feel ill".

I said, "I'm glad I don't have any germs". My brother laughed, "You can have some of mine then". He then wiped his hands all over me and it was disgusting.

However, as his hands came near my nose, I smelled the scent of soap. I knew that my brother must have washed his hands recently, which meant that I was safe from feeling ill.

I also realized that even though I didn't get any of my brother's germs, he might have picked some up from me so I had the last laugh in the end.

Count Dracula

I went on a vacation to Transylvania with my family. I was really excited and so too was my brother.

On the long journey, my brother was sharing facts, "Did you know that this is where Count Dracula lived?" I said, "Who's he?" My brother replied, "He's only the most powerful vampire to ever exist".

My brother went into great detail about how vampires suck people's blood. It put me right off my dinner.

When we finally got to our hotel, I saw a bat fly into the roof above my room and so did my brother. He teased, "Did you know that vampires can turn into bats?"

I pleaded with my brother, "Can we swap rooms?" He said, "No way. I called dibs first". He then left the room saying, "Sleep tight. Don't let the vampires bite".

I woke up in the morning and I noticed that my bedroom window was open. I was sure that I shut it at night but I didn't think too much of it until I looked in the mirror and saw two fang marks on my neck.

I thought that a vampire had sucked some of my blood in the night. I then tried to wash it off and I realized that it was just two red pen marks. Thank goodness it wasn't a permanent marker pen. No guess for who had drawn on me either...

Octopus

My dad took my brother and me to the local swimming pool and it was packed full of people.

Before my dad left us to sit on a bench to watch us swim, he told us that we could go and visit an aquarium afterwards. I said, "That would be awesome".

Just as I got into the swimming pool, my older brother chose this moment to tell me that he had heard that an octopus had escaped from the aquarium.

He continued to say, "One of the most fascinating things about an octopus is that it can squeeze through any gap as long as it is no smaller than one of its eyes".

I looked at a water vent and it was much bigger than an octopus's eye. This got me worrying.

My brother didn't seem fussed though and he continued to swim underwater. When he didn't pop up to surface for ages, I started to worry that the escaped octopus had got him.

I looked around and then this great big octopus leapt out of the water and landed on my face. Luckily, I managed to fight it off me.

However, when I noticed that the octopus was floating on the water, I realized that it was just an inflatable toy. It was also a lot of fun to play with, much more fun than my brother!

Voodoo doll

My mother is really good at using a sewing machine. She has used it to repair lots of things such as the holes I frequently ripped in my socks, the stretched neckline of one of my t-shirts and she has even fixed my coat after I unraveled the stitching on the sleeves.

As she was patching up the knees of my jeans, I noticed that next to her on the table she had a doll with lots of pins in it. I asked her if I could play with it but it made my mom make a sewing mistake.

She shouted, "Now look what you made me do". I said, "Sorry". However, it didn't feel like I was forgiven as she aggressively unpicked the stitching.

My brother bent his index finger to call me over. He said, "Oh, you are in so much trouble". I said, "I only wanted to play with the doll. By the way, do you know why it has so many pins in it?"

My brother said, "Isn't it obvious. It's a Voodoo doll". I was puzzled because I have not heard of that type of doll before.

My brother explained to me, "It is a new type of punishment that our mom has got planned for us. You see, if she pokes the right arm of the Voodoo doll with a pin, then it will make you feel pain in your right arm too".

I didn't like the sound of this new type of punishment. So I went to snatch the Voodoo doll off my mom's table.

However, when my mom pulled a pin out of the doll and used the pin for her sewing, I realized that it wasn't a voodoo doll - it was just a pincushion. I'm glad I didn't take it away or else my mom would have never finished fixing my jeans.

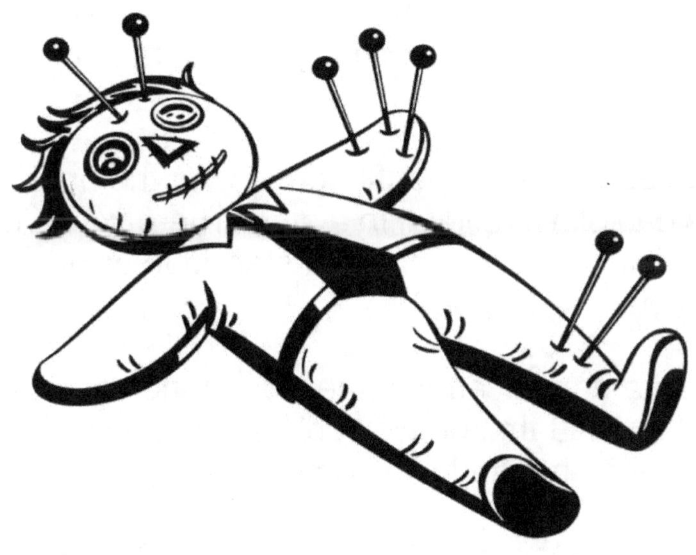

Bandit

My dad took our family on a car trip. I was in the back seat with my annoying brother who kept saying, "Are we there yet?"

Eventually my dad got so sick of replying, "Not yet" that he told my mom, "Right, "I'm going to take the quicker route". My mom hesitated, "Are you sure?"

He made a turn and as I looked out of the side window, I saw beautiful green scenery and a large bridge stretching over a wide blue river.

I liked this quicker route already and I didn't understand why my mom had doubts about taking this route. It seemed perfect, maybe too perfect.

Just as we were about to drive over the bridge, my dad slowed down to a stop. There weren't any cars in front of him so I started to wonder why he had stopped.

Then a bandit came to the side of the car and told my dad that he wouldn't let him pass unless he handed him some money.

I asked my brother, "What's going on?" He replied, "I think we're being robbed".

My dad paid the ransom by handing the bandit some notes and coins. After the bandit counted the money, he waved my dad forward.

As my dad drove on the bridge, I looked through the back window and I realized that it wasn't a bandit at all - it was just a toll road. My dad still called it daylight robbery though.

Box monster

It was my birthday and I had a big pile of presents that I couldn't wait to open. Once everyone was in the room, I tore through the wrappers and I threw them up into the air for Scooby to play in.

After I thought I had opened everything, my brother handed me a present that was hidden behind his back. He said, "This one is from me".

The wrapper was sealed with lots of tape and I had to seriously peck at it to get it all off. After I finally unwrapped it, my brother said, "Whatever you do, do not open the cardboard box".

I questioned, "Why not?" He replied, "Because I managed to catch a real monster but if you open the box then it will get out".

I started to think of the presents that he had given me in the past. Last year he got me a box of chocolates with all of the nice ones eaten. The year before that he gave me a load of junk and every year before then has been just as bad.

It made me think, "Hang on a minute. He's just got me an empty box and told me to not open it so that I wouldn't find out he's got me nothing. This is the worst present ever".

I had to make sure that I was right before I accused my brother of anything that bad. So I went to take just a little peek inside. But out of the tiniest crack, a monster jumped out towards my face.

However, when I saw that the monster was attached to a spring, I quickly realized that it was not a real monster at all – it was just a Jack-in-the-box toy. It was also the best present my brother has given me.

Scarecrow

Whilst I was walking through a cornfield with my brother, he pointed at a scarecrow that he had spotted. This old looking scarecrow had a worn out hat and he carried a dusty handbag.

There were also lots of crows flying around and one crow even decided to perch on the scarecrow's arm.

My brother laughed, "Aren't scarecrows supposed to scare crows?" I laughed at the scarecrow too and said, "That old thing is never going to scare anything".

I think I spoke too soon though because the scarecrow started to come to life. First, it's head twitched and then it's arm started to move.

The crow sitting on the scarecrow's arm was the first to fly away. It also spooked all of the other crows away too.

My brother said in a scared voice, "We should get out of here". I agreed but we were both so scared that we were frozen to the spot.

However, when something jumped out of the scarecrow, I realized that the scarecrow wasn't alive - it was just a little mouse that was living inside the straw.

I said, "Who would have thought that something so small could scare us all?" My brother denied being scared but I knew the truth.

Frankenstein monster

I was sitting on a chair and I was watching my mother make a patchwork quilt out of scrap bits of material.

Then all of a sudden; every light in the house went out. My mom said, "Don't worry, it must be a power cut. I'll go fetch some candles".

I was left alone in the dark with my brother who told me, "A power cut can be caused by someone using too much electricity in one go". He continued to say, "Hey, didn't Frankenstein's monster need a lot of electricity to come back to life?"

My brother always knew how to scare me. I started to think that my dad was doing one of his biological experiments in our basement.

I wanted to be ready to run so I stood up but as I did so, I heard something drop on to the floor. I picked it up and it felt like a nut.

I recalled that Frankenstein's monster had a bolt in his neck and I thought that maybe his nut had come loose.

When my mom found the candles, it lit up the room and I sat back down on my chair.

However, I noticed that my chair was now wobbly and then I realized that the nut didn't come out of Frankenstein's monster's neck - it had come out of my chair. I was just worrying over nothing.

Genie

My granddad had come out of hospital and he came to visit us. He also brought with him a really old looking lamp.

I said, "Wow, is that one of those lamps with a genie inside?" My granddad looked at the dull metal lamp for a moment and he said, "Yes".

I was so excited that I immediately started to think about the 3 wishes that I wanted.

I pleaded, "Can I rub the lamp?" He said, "Sure". He handed me the lamp and he said, "The lamp can be a bit rough on your fingers so I recommend using this cloth".

After rubbing the lamp both clockwise and anti-clockwise, I said, "It's not doing anything". My granddad said, "Perhaps you have to rub it in the right spot".

I rubbed every square inch of the lamp with the cloth that he gave me and there was still no sign of a genie. I handed it back to my granddad and I said, "I think it's broken".

He held the lamp and admired its beautiful shiny surface and he said, "No, it's perfect".

Then I realized that there was never any genie inside - it was just my granddad fooling me into polishing his lamp. He can be very crafty at times. I wonder if my brother takes after him.

Dungeon

My brother asked me if I wanted a Chinese burn. I didn't know what it was but I said, "OK". He then grabbed hold of my arm and twisted it in opposite directions. It really hurt so I hurt him back by giving him a nipple cripple.

It didn't end there though because we gave each other monkey rubs, wedgies and a flat foot.

My dad saw what we were doing to each other and he didn't like it. He shouted, "That's it. I'm taking you both to the dungeon". I pleaded, "I'll be good, I promise".

My dad raised his voice, "Put your shoes on, we're going and that's that". We then got into his car and my brother moaned, "This is your fault". I argued, "But you started it". My dad said, "And I'm finishing it".

I stayed quiet until my brother whispered, "I wonder what punishment our dad has got planned for us". I whispered back, "I don't want to know".

My brother told me all of the different things that happen inside a dungeon and it scared me stiff.

However, when we finally got there, I realized that it wasn't a real dungeon - it was just a dungeon museum. Phew, what a relief.

Tornado

One day, Scooby was acting very odd. He kept barking at me and then he started to shake in fear before finding a hiding space under my bed. He even refused to come out for a treat, which was not like him at all.

I told my mom and dad about Scooby's strange behavior but they just thought that Scooby wanted some attention. I on the other hand knew that something was wrong because nobody knows Scooby better than me.

As I was thinking what the problem was, my brother came into my room and he said, "Dogs can sense things that humans can't you know". I said, "Yes, you're right. What do you think Scooby is sensing?"

My brother stroked his chin and replied, "Since he is under cover, I'm guessing that he's sensing a tornado is on its way to our house. I'm only 99% percent certain though, with a 1% chance that it is an earthquake, tsunami or volcano instead".

I said, "So either way, we're doomed then?" My brother provided me with little comfort by saying, "I'm afraid so". He then walked away saying, "It's been nice knowing you".

I waited to see which environmental disaster would strike first. When I heard a constant rumbling noise that was getting louder, I knew that my brother was right in thinking that it was a tornado.

At one point, the noise was so loud that it felt like the tornado was over my house. But nothing was blowing around. So I looked out of the window and I realized that it wasn't a tornado - it was a military airplane flying low to the ground over our house.

Goblin

I went to visit the town with my family and we saw a goblin. My dad said, "Hey, that's not something you see everyday is it?"

My brother stupidly rushed forward to get a closer look at the goblin but I hung back for obvious safety reasons.

This green goblin was left-handed and it had a sword. As it stood on the spot, it was tempting people to come closer to it. When they were close enough, the goblin swung its sword at them.

Luckily, the goblin missed every time. I cried to my mom, "I don't like it. Somebody's going to get hurt. I want to go home".

My mom put her arm around me and she said, "It's all right. There's nothing to worry about".

My brother was now standing really close to the goblin and I dreaded what the goblin was going to do to him.

The goblin spun on the spot and its sword went around in a full circle. Then the goblin fell on to the floor because it must have got dizzy.

We then walked towards my brother and I noticed that above the goblin, there was some string hanging down from a window.

I then realized that it wasn't a real goblin - it was just a string puppet and I'm so glad that it cut its own strings because now it won't be scaring any more children.

Fortune teller

I was with my dad at a psychic fair and he asked me what I wanted to be when I grew up. I told him, "I want to do something that I like and I do like to play doctor".

I continued talking, "With my toy set, I am already able to check someone's pulse, take a temperature reading and put a plaster on someone.

My dad smiled, "I think you will make a wonderful doctor".

I looked at my stuffed teddy bears that I was carrying with me and I said, "I think so too. Maybe even the best doctor in the world as I have managed to cure all of my teddies".

We then sat at a table with a lady who said she could read my future. She had a deck of Tarot cards and she asked me to pick a card.

When I flipped the card over, I was horrified because it was the Death card. I looked at my teddies and I started to panic, "Which one's going to die?"

The lady then explained that the Death card didn't literally mean death. Instead it meant the end of one thing and the start of another.

I wondered what it could mean and then I realized that it must have been referring to the end of one school and the start of another school. It was certainly something that made me scared, especially since I was going to start in the big school soon.

Pirate

Friday the 13th is believed by many to be the unluckiest day of them all. On that day, I was on a rowing boat with my big brother.

I sat at the front of the boat whilst my brother did all of the rowing. He stopped rowing for a moment and asked, "Have you heard about the pirate that sailed in these waters?"

I replied, "Nobody has told me about that". He explained, "It's probably because you're too young to hear it".

This only made me want to know it more. I pleaded, "You've got to tell me now". He said, "Oh all right then, if you insist".

My brother put on a different ascent as he told me, "It is said that a pirate called Smallbeard stole so much treasure that it sunk his ship. Now he swims around all day looking for a new boat to commandeer".

Since I was in a boat that Smallbeard wanted, it made me nervous. As I looked into the water, the boat suddenly started to rock.

I thought, "Oh no, Smallbeard is trying to climb onboard. This really is an unlucky day".

However, when I looked behind me, I realized that it was just my brother rocking the boat. I told him, "One of these days, I'm going to get you back".

Dragon

My school has a pet hamster and my friends and I often looked after it. One day whilst feeding the hamster, I got talking to my friends Sam and Riley about what pets they had.

Riley said, "I don't have any pets because my mom is allergic to them". Sam then surprised us both by saying, "Well I've got a dragon".

I was shocked, "No way". Sam grinned and said, "Yes way. It is only a little one but the shopkeeper told me that it will grow a lot bigger one day".

Riley asked, "Can it breathe fire?" Sam replied, "I haven't seen it breathe fire yet but that's only because I don't give my dragon any reason to get mad with me".

Sam asked me if I wanted to see the dragon. I said, "Yes please, he sounds awesome" and so we went to Sam's house after school.

Before seeing the dragon, Sam said, "Whatever you do, don't do anything to make my dragon mad".

I was incredibly nervous to see the dragon now.
However, when I did hold it, the dragon looked
at me with big eyes and I laughed as the little
dragon licked me.

I knew that it was hungry, but also that it
couldn't hurt me. I had by now realized that it
was a bearded dragon lizard and I knew that
they were totally harmless and didn't breathe
fire. But they are very cute!

Living trees

I was in the woods with my brother and I was building a stick fort, while he was busy climbing trees.

Eventually when my brother came down from a tree, he took one look at my fort and he told me, "Should you be doing that?" I replied, "I'm not doing anything wrong am I?"

He said, "It's just that trees are living things and you have taken away pieces of them".

I reasoned, "It's perfectly fine because I've only taken the dead wood that has already fallen to the ground".

My brother stroked his chin and asked, "But do all of the trees know that?" I replied, "No because trees don't have eyes".

My brother said, "Some do". He then carried one of the logs that I had collected and he said, "I had better give it back to the tree before it gets angry".

Moments later, he shouted, "Help, the tree is eating me". I thought, "Oh no, this is my fault. It was me who made the trees angry".

I rushed over to save my brother whom I noticed was already half way inside the tree. I knew I didn't have long to save him so I reacted by grabbing hold of his new sweater and I pulled as hard as I could.

When I finally managed to pull my brother to safety, I realized that the tree was hollow. My brother tricked me but his trick backfired on himself because his new sweater was now torn.

T-Rex

My dad knew how much I liked dinosaurs and since he was a biology teacher, I asked him if it was possible to bring them back to life.

My dad said, "It is certainly possible but it is very unlikely to happen any time soon".

The thought of one day seeing a real life dinosaur such as a Triceratops eating leaves from the trees in my garden set my imagination running.

Then my brother said, "I hope they make a T-Rex in the future". I argued, "But they eat all of the dinosaurs that I like". He grinned, "And that's why I like them".

He then teased me for being a vegetarian and said that I was at the bottom of the food chain.

I complained to my dad, "My brother's being mean AGAIN". However, my dad didn't do anything about it. All he said was, "What goes around comes around".

This got me thinking that it was time that I should play a trick on my brother to see how he liked it.

So when he went to get a snack, I hid behind the door. Then when he came back into the room, I roared as loud as a T-Rex.

He squeezed his eyes shut and when he finally did open one of them, he realized that there wasn't a T-Rex in the house – it was me who had scared him. I laughed loudly, "I told you I'd get you back".